CREATIVE IDEAS FOR

GARDEN DECORATION

CREATIVE IDEAS FOR

GARDEN DECORATION

PRACTICAL ADVICE ON ADDING INTEREST
TO OUTDOOR SPACES, WITH CONTAINERS,
STATUES, WATER FEATURES AND ORNAMENTS

JENNY HENDY

southwater

This edition is published by Southwater,
an imprint of Anness Publishing Ltd,
Hermes House, 88–89 Blackfriars Road,
London SE1 8HA;
tel. 020 7401 2077;
fax 020 7633 9499

www.southwaterbooks.com;
www.annesspublishing.com

If you like the images in this book and would
like to investigate using them for publishing,
promotions or advertising, please visit our website
www.practicalpictures.com for more information.

UK agent: The Manning Partnership Ltd;
tel. 01225 478444; fax 01225 478440;
sales@manning-partnership.co.uk
UK distributor: Grantham Book Services Ltd;
tel. 01476 541080; fax 01476 541061;
orders@gbs.tbs-ltd.co.uk
North American agent/distributor: National
Book Network; tel. 301 459 3366;
fax 301 429 5746; www.nbnbooks.com
Australian agent/distributor: Pan Macmillan Australia;
tel. 1300 135 113; fax 1300 135 103;
customer.service@macmillan.com.au
New Zealand agent/distributor: David Bateman Ltd;
tel. (09) 415 7664; fax (09) 415 8892

Publisher: Joanna Lorenz
Managing Editor: Judith Simons
Senior Editor: Sarah Ainley
Designer: Louise Clements
Indexer: Helen Snaith
Production Controller: Stephen Lang

ETHICAL TRADING POLICY

Because of our ongoing ecological investment
programme, you, as our customer, can have the
pleasure and reassurance of knowing that a tree is
being cultivated on your behalf to naturally replace
the materials used to make the book you are holding.
For further information about this scheme, go to
www.annesspublishing.com/trees

Previously published as *Garden Ornament*

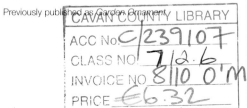

contents

introduction

Ever since gardens were first created for pleasure, decorative elements have played an essential role. In ancient Greek, Roman and Persian gardens, for example, there would have been formal pools and fountains, finely carved stonework, ornate tiles and mosaics, wall paintings and topiary. In many ways, little has changed as far as what constitutes decorative features, but we are now able to select from a staggering range of ornaments that span every historical period. Nature, too, provides inspiration for garden decoration.

Decorative elements may be purchased direct from stores, garden centres, craft centres, artists' studios and salvage yards, as well as over the internet. You can also acquire the skills to create your own: willow weaving, mosaic art, stained glass work and so on. But this doesn't always make the question of what to buy any easier to answer. Do you try to match the style or period of the house; would it be better to make a radical departure and create a whole new look for the garden; how about different looks to distinguish or separate areas?

Occasionally, a single ornament will dictate the style of a whole garden, but more often it is the other way around, and decoration is something of an afterthought. Garden ornaments can be expensive, and it pays to take time over your selection. Sketch out your ideas and scan through books and magazines, taking clippings of images that you like. Ask yourself what it is about them that appeals to your personal aesthetic sense.

This book embraces tradition, but it also adopts a modern standpoint and aims to encourage flexibility and invention when it comes to adding garden ornaments. The book is divided into two richly illustrated sections: the first section explains how to set the stage for features so that they assume the proper significance, while the second is an inspirational review of the materials that can be used, including man-made and natural elements, as well as sculptural plants.

ABOVE: *This pair of cordylines are ornamental in their own right, and they also begin a framing process that is continued by the arched walkway and leads to a view of the open countryside beyond.*

LEFT: *A wind chime suspended from a tree branch makes an interesting detail, and the soft harmonies that it produces will add a new and inviting sound dimension to your garden.*

RIGHT: *Water flows elegantly over this wall-mounted cast-iron lily pad. The sound of trickling water will enhance any outdoor space, and an ornamental feature such as this, attached to a wall, need not take up an inordinate amount of space.*

The key to success with garden ornaments is knowing where and how to place them

No matter how beautiful an object or a piece of sculpture, the decorative effect cannot be fully appreciated unless it has the right setting. And some elements only become ornamental when they are removed from their usual environment, grouped with others and relocated imaginatively.

There are all kinds of considerations to be aware of when deciding on the perfect position for an object. Are you aiming for maximum drama, or do you favour a more subtle approach? The latter can be far more evocative and help to mask any faults or shortcomings that the object may have.

If you're working with a large, heavy element it pays to do the groundwork first. Experiment using a plastic dustbin or pile of cardboard boxes as a stand-in for a large urn, for example. Alternatively, take snap shots and sketch the item in various locations until you find a position you're happy with.

vistas & sight lines

A little knowledge of perspective goes a long way towards placing ornaments successfully, and this is especially true if you are planning a formal garden setting, where the margin of error is much smaller.

In a formal garden, you can utilize the straight lines of paths, borders, rectangular pools or rills, and lawns to direct the eye towards a particular feature. Standing at one end of a pathway for example, the lines appear to converge towards a vanishing point in the distance, and this illusion can be used to focus the eye and draw it towards a point of your choice. You can emphasize the significance of a pathway by lining it with low-clipped hedging punctuated by taller topiary shapes or identically potted plants. On a long straight route that bisects the plot, you could have several points of interest. For example, you could set up a feature midway along, such as a sundial positioned at the centre of a circle of paving and, at the end of the path, perhaps an arbour or summerhouse, where you could sit and enjoy the view in the other direction.

The points where paths cross or come to a T-junction; significant changes in level, such as a flight of steps; entrances to garden "rooms" of distinct character: these are all design features that can be strengthened with an appropriately placed ornament or decorative element. Paired objects such as matching topiaries, metal obelisks or stone vases emphasize symmetry and raise the perceived level of importance of doors and entrance ways. However, bear in mind that each feature should be separated visually from the next, otherwise the focus will be distracted and the impact lost.

LEFT: *Perfectly lined up, these arch-shaped apertures focus the view through to the far bench. Precise symmetry is the key here, and when planning this kind of feature, it's a good idea to use parallel rows of bamboo canes as makeshift surveying poles.*

RIGHT: *An avenue of identically shaped trees or clipped topiary shapes can gently lead the eye towards a focal point. In this intriguing Eastern-influenced design, still reflecting pools bisect the main axis, creating a landscape of shapes and reflections.*

In a small garden you might not feel there is room to take advantage of sight lines, but you can fool the visitor into thinking that the plot is much longer by making the lines of a path or lawn converge. The effect can be magnified by using smaller pieces of paving towards the vanishing point or by reducing the size of plants along the path. Colours can also become more muted, with hot vibrant shades near the house and soft greys, blues and purples – the colour of distant hills – further away. The final touch is to place an ornamental feature at the end of the path, in scale with the illusion. Urns and vases, statuary and pedestals come in a wide range of sizes so this shouldn't be a problem, but it is advisable to experiment first with stacked cardboard boxes to get a feeling for the dimensions required.

By keeping the boundaries of the plot a secret and only allowing glimpsed views through selected apertures, you can maintain a high level of drama and make the garden feel much larger. Internal hedges, walls and screens that block the view of other areas as you explore the garden are the answer. If you are more ambitious, you could create covered walkways and pergolas along sections of pathway or *allées* of pleached lime. Of course, you must provide some kind of visual rewards for the visitor, otherwise they will feel disappointment every

ABOVE LEFT: *All this lavender-lined pathway lacks is a suitable end point – a rustic bench beneath the apple tree, perhaps.*

ABOVE RIGHT: *This is a wonderful example of grand theatre, with giant yew pyramids flanking an immaculately mown lawn and leading the eye first to a set of imposing gateposts and finally to the building at the far end.*

LEFT: *Bold blue fencing and a beach-like sweep of gravel draw attention to the old rowing boat – an intriguing garden feature in its own right.*

time they reach a potential viewing point; this is where ornamental elements come into their own.

In a more relaxed garden setting, you can afford to adopt quite a subtle approach in the way you position objects. Curving or meandering pathways still lead the eye, but the lack of symmetry means that you have greater freedom in placing a sculpture or ornament. For example, you could offset the object, placing it within the border or to one side of an entrance way. You can set up staggered screens of trellis or planting to block the view down an S-shaped lawn or pathway and use the hidden areas around each bend to create suspense. The viewer should be kept guessing as to what delights they might discover around the next corner.

Part of the art of gardening is to keep something back –
if you can see the whole garden, the magic is gone

framing

Much of the process of placing ornaments successfully is concerned with building pictures. How you frame a scene is the all-important part: the trick is to include only what you want to be seen.

Creating a framed setting involves selecting a particular object or grouping, and then deliberately blocking out any extraneous parts of the view. These could be anything that distract from the main focus, such as an eyesore or something that overcomplicates the composition.

Every time we look at the garden through a window, we are observing it through a frame. It pays to observe the garden from key positions in the house, such as the kitchen or an armchair close to a French window, so that you can work out how best to put the focus on the main features. Ask yourself what areas you might need to screen in order to enhance a particular element.

Examples of man-made garden frames include archways, arbours and gazebos. For archways to work successfully, you need to fill in the gaps on either side of the arch, or at least baffle the eye with trellis panels or planting. Otherwise you can end up looking to either side of the frame and the impact is lost. It is perfectly acceptable to place an archway within a border or in the corner of a garden simply to add emphasis to a feature sited there, a bench seat perhaps, or a sculpted figure. Again, use planting to draw the structure into the fabric of the garden and make it look less staged and conspicuous.

A narrow gap cut through dense hedging can create a sense of mystery, giving a tantalizing glimpse of the garden on the other side. The view might be of hot red and orange blooms, a cooling fountain or the wild landscape beyond.

A frame such as an open doorway in a garden wall might completely surround the object in question, but framing can be much more subtle. For example, you could take advantage of the arching branches of a tree or shrub and place a ceramic vase in the space below. Similarly, when you have an ornament set in a lawn or paved area, a low-level planting of herbaceous flowers, grasses or ferns will provide a soft framework or setting.

TOP LEFT: *Arches and pergola walkways are excellent tools for framing a particular view, an ornamental feature or simply another area of the garden, as here. By covering them with trained shrubs, fruit trees or climbers, such as roses, you can create a tunnel of greenery that will focus the eye.*

BOTTOM LEFT: *A floral arbour makes a subtle but decorative frame for a piece of statuary, creating a theatrical effect in a quiet corner of the garden. The roses, foxgloves and clematis make perfect stage curtains for this thoughtful stone "player".*

RIGHT: *Imposing gateposts topped with finials make a grand entrance to this formal garden, with its long central axis and symmetrical features. The pair of large clipped topiary domes are equally effective at framing the view at the midway point, maintaining the interest en route to the shaded bench.*

rhythm & repetition

Against the seemingly chaotic backdrop of flower and foliage, the eye immediately picks out the geometric shapes and regular patterns of deliberately contrived features, which impose a sense of order.

Repeating identical elements in a rhythmical way can create strong, dynamic features. One relatively small object on its own will have minimal impact, but repeated at set intervals in a straight line or following a curve or the rim of a circle, the decorative effect multiplies dramatically.

Solid elements with a simple outline, such as clipped yew pyramids or stone spheres, work particularly well in formal settings, defining key lines and points on the ground plan. But you could use something as basic as matching pots or containers to set up a rhythm on a terrace, around a garden pond, down a flight of steps or along a pathway.

For even greater sculptural impact try planting larger pots with standards, creating rows of marguerites, fuchsias, *Hydrangea paniculata* or tightly clipped topiary standards of box, holly or *Ligustrum delavayanum*. Placed at regular intervals within the flower border, these can add height, structure and form without the effect seeming too rigid and overwhelming. For a softer look in a country or cottage garden or formal potager, try using willow or trellis obelisks in the same way.

Concave trellis panels may be used to create a visual rhythm along a boundary – top the posts with decorative finials for extra emphasis. You could achieve a similar look using a line of posts connected by heavy loops of rope that have been smothered or softened with rambler roses or clematis.

TOP LEFT: *Circular stepping-stones made from log slices create a pleasing curve through this lush bog garden.*

LEFT: *A chequerboard design makes an eye-catching substitute for a flat expanse of paving. Add giant ceramic chess pieces for a finishing touch.*

RIGHT: *In this extension of the potager, where fruits, vegetables and herbs are arranged for decorative effect, tightly clipped* Santolina *balls have been laid out to form a regular ground pattern and are rhythmically punctuated by obelisks, on which the garden produce is being trained.*

raising your sights

Lifting a small ornament off the ground and placing it on a low wall, table or flight of steps raises its prominence significantly. You could also mount the object on a wall or hang it from a tree branch.

One particularly effective method of focusing attention on a decorative object is to raise the item on a pedestal or plinth. Depending on the ornament, this could be as simple as a stone gatepost, a stump of tree trunk or a stout piece of reclaimed timber.

Flat pieces of slate stacked on top of one another and rotated to create a rough cylinder would also work, as would a pile of old bricks or breezeblocks, wired together for stability and rendered with cement for a smooth finish. You could even use a disused drainpipe topped with a small paving slab, although the paving slab and the object would need to be firmly secured. To exhibit a bust or stone urn in a period setting, you would probably use a plinth shaped like a Greek or Roman column, but contemporary art needs a platform that won't conflict with the style or material of construction. Finally, if you have a suitable "window" or aperture in a garden wall, this makes a wonderful place for displaying coloured glass.

TOP LEFT: *This rustic bird cage looks just right suspended from a tree branch. Lanterns also work well in this situation.*

LEFT: *Perfectly in character, a cheeky fox taunts the garden owners as it runs along the top of the boundary wall. Look out for ornaments designed for wall display.*

ABOVE: *A rusting cast-iron vase is suitably mellow in appearance for this waterside location, and raised up on an old stone plinth, it speaks of faded elegance. Notice how the plain green foliage backdrop really brings the decorative detail and colouring into focus.*

floor work

One of the ways to make a more significant position for a garden ornament, be it a statue, sculptural plant or collection of pots, is to create a pattern at its base that will provide a framework and setting.

Most types of flooring can be quite easily worked up into something more decorative. For instance, you might have a large terracotta pot at the centre of a Mediterranean-style gravel garden. Here, you could enhance the ornamental value of the pot further by laying down a square of colourful gemstones that will twinkle in the hot midday sun. Another example is in a herb garden, where you could use clipped box or dwarf lavender to create a mini hedge around a fountain or sundial. Within a uniformly paved area, it is a good idea to lift the paving surrounding the ornament and replace it with a contrasting material, such as cobbles set into concrete or pantiles laid on edge to create a sunburst design.

Stepping-stones can also be used to direct the eye towards an object. The Japanese are past masters at this technique, increasing the size of the stones and setting them closer together as they near the object. The final stone is always large enough to stand on to contemplate the object.

ABOVE: *Jewel-like glass beads create a feeling of unity at the base of this Mediterranean pot collection.*

TOP RIGHT: *A gravel circle planted with alpines gives greater emphasis to the central ornament. For a formal alternative, edge plain gravel with a low-clipped hedge.*

RIGHT: *Mosaics of pebbles, cobbles, stone shards and even pieces of broken ceramic are easy to assemble and make a wonderful feature in their own right. Here a starburst design helps to unite a loose grouping of terracotta pots.*

colour backdrops

If there is insufficient contrast between an ornament and its surroundings, the ornament will simply blend in. Being creative with colour is also a key way to add drama or to generate an atmosphere.

The degree of contrast you decide on will depend on how striking an effect you wish to achieve. If you're looking for a subtle enhancement, you might select a toning colour. For example, you could place a terracotta pot against a wall painted dusty apricot. But for maximum drama you might take the plunge and opt for a shade of purple or blue, which are on the opposite side to orange on the artist's colour wheel.

As is often the case in the garden, away from the house, you may not have a suitably positioned wall or fence that could be painted to provide a backdrop. If so, you could simply surround the decorative element with flowers or foliage of an appropriate shade – golden yellow leaves or blooms for a blue glazed jar, perhaps rich green for an ornament or structure painted lacquer-red. Another option would be to place a piece of trellis or a panel of canvas as a colour screen to enhance an object in the foreground.

Blocks of solid colour can operate like abstract art in the garden, influencing the mood and energy levels of the space. This is worth bearing in mind when you come to repaint a wall, door or garden building. For example, might you be able to enhance the view from the window by choosing something other than white for a key section of a sunny courtyard? What about painting one wall in a warm earth tone, such as deep red-brown, and using that as a backdrop for a dazzling blue mosaic-framed mirror or a row of lavender planted in shiny metal pails? White can be quite a difficult colour, being so stark and cold, and white furniture or pale grey stone ornaments tend to look best against a backdrop of cool greens and blues. Green topiary stands out well against a white backdrop, but a wash of cool lemon yellow might be more interesting.

Painted colour backdrops are inexpensive to create and provide pleasure all year round, even in winter when seasonal plants have died down. It is certainly fun to experiment!

TOP LEFT: *Clever use of colour backdrops can sometimes turn quite an ordinary arrangement into a highly effective focal point. To achieve this dusty pink colourwash, roughly brush over the base coat with a deeper shade.*

BOTTOM LEFT: *Starry blue campanulas form a cascade behind this little cherub fountain, demonstrating that flowers and foliage, as well as paint, can be used for creating colour backdrops. Clipped hedges of green- or gold-leafed plants work particularly well as a backdrop to red or blue ornaments.*

RIGHT: *Rendered walls are far easier to paint than raw brick or stone, and you can disguise cheap breezeblock constructions with cement and several applications of differently shaded colourwash to give the effect of faded plasterwork. In this Mediterranean-style courtyard, the backdrop adds a note of authenticity.*

tricks of the eye

Success with visual trickery is all about getting the detail right and using finishing touches to convince the viewer that the picture is real. Anything that adds to the three-dimensional quality is ideal.

It is possible to create the illusion of a passageway simply by fixing a false-perspective trellis panel to a wall, but the image is far more believable when the trellis edges are softened with foliage, and an ornament, such as a vase on a pedestal, is placed in front. Similarly, a mural showing a view beyond the garden wall would be much more successful if an old door frame was fixed around the outside of it.

One of the easiest ways to deceive the eye is to utilize reflections. Wall-mounted mirrors can trick the viewer into thinking that there is a way through to another garden, beyond the walls and fences, and like the false-perspective trellis panel and mural, they can make the space feel larger as a result. To completely fool the viewer you need to tilt the mirror to capture the most believable reflection, and to camouflage the edges, so that it doesn't seem like glass at all.

A pathway leading right up to the base of a mirror will create the illusion of a way through, and you can reinforce the doorway theme by framing the mirror with identical pots of topiary or other sentinel-like objects. With an old mirror, where the silvering has worn away to leave a less than perfect image, you could cut a piece of wood to frame the mirror and use this "doorway" to highlight a statue or urn raised on a plinth. Alternatively, if you can source an old wrought-iron gate, you could have a mirror cut to fit, and then all you'd have to do to convince someone that this was a way through to a secret garden would be to grow an unruly climber around it.

Perhaps the most subtle and persuasive way of using a mirror is simply to attach an old door – frame and all – to the wall, and then open the door slightly so that you just catch a glimpse of the reflection created by the mirror inside. Features like this seem to work particularly well when fixed to an ivy-clad wall or fence in the shade of overhanging trees, where natural shadows mask any imperfections.

LEFT: *This old wall mirror shrouded by firethorn and golden hop creates the illusion of a doorway that leads through the wall to another garden.*

ABOVE: *An ordinary wooden-slat garden gate looks like it leads from an alleyway to a mysterious garden beyond, with the twig wreath making the gate seem even more like a genuine access point – except that behind it is a solid brick wall.*

textural contrast

The more an object differs in appearance from its surroundings, the more it will stand out. Try to forget about colour and imagine the scene in black and white so that you can concentrate on the textures.

Man-made elements usually offer the greatest contrast to a backdrop of leaves and flowers because their texture and profile are so different from what we find in nature. Placing an object with a smooth, hard surface, such as a Greek pithos, among soft-textured plants, such as diaphanous grasses or feathery shuttlecock ferns, would make you all the more conscious of its solidity and pleasantly curved outline.

When siting an ornamental feature, look for leaf shapes and textures that differ dramatically from the material the object is made from. If the decorative element is smooth with a sheen or gloss, contrast that with something roughly textured or with a matt finish – perhaps a surface of slate shards or weathered timber, a backdrop of heather screening or jaggedly cut leaves with a felted texture. Conversely, when finding the best site for a rough-textured element, such as a standing stone, contrast it with a smooth, plain backdrop, such as a closely mown lawn, fine grit or a glossy leaved plant such as *Fatsia japonica*.

Objects bearing a subtle design or pattern, or a raised motif, and those with a delicate latticework construction also need to be positioned with care – nothing should be allowed to compete with the fine detail. The smooth architectural lines of formal hedging can make the perfect backdrop, especially in the form of dark, immaculately clipped yew. For small ornate elements, try mounting them on a plain rendered wall or setting them into smooth paving.

LEFT: *The smooth and solid nature of this contemporary sculpture is highlighted by the light, airy grasses behind that move with the slightest breeze. Awareness of different textures makes gardening a more sensual experience.*

RIGHT: *It can be hard to find a piece of sculpture to suit your garden, but large and simply decorated pots like these fit in almost anywhere. The smooth curves are very restful to look at and, set within a border, they make a lovely foil for foliage.*

lighting effects

During the day ornaments are illuminated by the sun and their colour shifts subtly as the quality of light changes from dawn till dusk. At night, the garden can be transformed with artificial lights.

Pale objects or those with a reflective surface may seem too bright in the glare of midday and yet these same objects glow or glimmer enticingly when placed in the shade. Dappled shade cast by trees, shrubs, grasses and bamboos offers some interesting daytime possibilities. Conversely, pieces with a heavy relief pattern or an interesting texture look best in sunlight, when shadows highlight all the chinks and crevices.

Moonlight supported by the soft glow of candles creates a wonderful ambience after sundown, but certain decorative elements require a special kind of lighting to really bring them into focus. The garden can be given a completely different look at night with artificial lighting and you can continue to enjoy views of your outdoor room even when the weather is too cold to dine alfresco. For theatrical drama, you need to make the most of the contrast between light and shadow, and this can be achieved by directing a focused light source at key objects and structures. These may not be particularly noticeable during the day, but with skilful positioning of the rays they could undergo a startling transformation at night.

Gardeners are now able to buy a wide range of discrete outdoor lighting fixtures from larger do-it-yourself stores, and these include mini spotlights that either attach to a structure or peg into the ground. Experiment first, setting the light at different angles before attaching it permanently. Uplighting from an angle usually produces pleasing results, and there is less of a problem with glare than when the light is wall-mounted and angled downwards. Small floodlights are more powerful than spots and are useful for highlighting the structure of tall trees and large, architectural shrubs. Be bold when illuminating statues and plants, and consider using a coloured light source every now and then. In courtyards, the well-defined shadows cast on to walls behind illuminated ornamental features or sculptural plants adds considerably to the visual excitement.

TOP LEFT: *Outdoor lanterns come in many shapes and sizes and you can create a wonderfully evocative atmosphere when a number of them are lit around the garden. Hang them from tree branches or hanging basket brackets attached to walls, or set them into wall niches.*

BOTTOM LEFT: *Church candles set in plain terracotta pots half sunk into the ground can be used to subtly light up a patio or pathway. These pots have been gilded and mixed with cobbles and would create a magical atmosphere beside a pool.*

RIGHT: *By carefully selecting from a wide range of lighting elements you can create almost any look, from subtle to dramatic. If there is no convenient outdoor electricity supply, use candle lanterns or individual solar-powered lights, which can be built into walls or positioned in shrubbery, as well as placed at the foot of ornaments.*

vignettes

Sometimes decorative elements are not strong enough to create a feature on their own, but when combined with other objects, materials and plants they become part of a pleasing picture.

One reason for creating a vignette is to display a personal themed collection in an attractive manner. This could be anything from a beachcomber's eccentric hoard to a collection of antique clay pots or garden tools. You can derive tremendous pleasure from composing these pictures, and you will learn much about colour, form and texture in the process. Think of it as creating a still-life painting in 3D. For smaller items, you might make your arrangement on a window ledge or stepped bench, which is how collections of the ornamental Japanese plants, bonsai, are often displayed.

Unless the items are vibrantly shaded, vignettes tend to work best with a relatively plain backdrop, or when contained or anchored by walls and buildings, otherwise surrounding plantings conflict. Toning colours will help to unite a random grouping, and don't forget that the colour and texture of the backdrop is also important.

Ring the changes and introduce a seasonal note by adding living material such as flower arrangements, potted bulbs, fruits and berries, harking back to childhood and the school nature table; children will enjoy making their own contributions. For special occasions, dress the scene with candles and sumptuous fabrics; items such as patterned tiles or old crockery may be added to enhance textural richness.

LEFT: *Pieces of architectural salvage can make intriguing elements for decorating the garden. Here a disparate grouping of antique metal has been brought together for dramatic effect.*

TOP RIGHT: *A collection of old gardening tools can be used as a display, as here, in a recreation of a Victorian potting bench.*

RIGHT: *Elegant trellis panels add an air of refinement to this collection of conservatory specimens and period planters.*

The fabric or substance that an ornamental object is made from has an immediate influence on the impression it creates.

Certain materials and finishes suggest a particular style. Unglazed terracotta, for example, conjures up visions of the Mediterranean and has classical overtones. Stainless steel and chrome say hi-tech urban living rather than rambling cottage garden, while woven wicker sculptures bring to mind country living. However, in reality the rules are not so hard and fast, and in contemporary garden design the boundaries are blurred. Part of the fun is bringing traditional materials into unconventional settings and putting an innovative twist on things. In a modern town garden you might have smooth slate paving and recycled timber seats, wicker baskets planted with geometric topiary, or classical cast-iron urns painted cornflower blue. In a country garden, you could find contemporary sculpture languishing in the long grass.

materials

ceramic

The warm tones of traditional terracotta bring to mind the heat, culture and relaxed way of life of the Mediterranean. Glazed ceramic has a totally different feel, and evokes exotic locations of the East.

The look and feel of terracotta pots and ornaments varies tremendously according to the type of clay, the way it has been fired and the overall design and decor. In larger garden centres you'll find everything from raw, hand-thrown pieces to classically inspired statuary and giant pots with intricate mouldings – these are perfect for the terrace of a Tuscan villa or to show off your specimen topiary. Formal terracotta associates well with dressed stone, brick and gravel and comes to life with a backdrop of dark green clipped hedging or trellis screening stained a soft blue-grey.

Being porous, terracotta weathers easily and after a while your new acquisitions will begin to look aged, blending in much more readily with the organic surroundings of the garden. Salts begin to work their way to the surface and a dusting of green algae will soon appear on pots that are positioned in shade. Some pots are smoked during the firing, which blackens the surface, or they can be part-glazed to give a rustic appearance. Using artist's acrylic paints, you can apply a diluted white colourwash for an instant weathered look, or sponge green shades around the contours of any decorative moulding to give the impression of algae. Paints are available for pot decoration, and adding a splash of colour can be a fun way to transform a collection of inexpensive clay pots. Another trick is to rub stove black into the surface, which results in a chic charcoal-grey metallic sheen.

To avoid having to water a planted pot so frequently, line the inside of pots with plastic before planting, leaving drainage holes at the bottom. Unless there is a frostproof guarantee, you may need to empty out vulnerable pots and store them under cover for the winter, or pack them round with insulation material, but in milder areas you can often get away with just moving pots up against the house. Place "feet" underneath to ensure good winter drainage.

LEFT: *Fired clay may look too new initially, but a certain amount of dampness and shade soon begins the natural weathering process.*

RIGHT: *For a bright and cheerful patio feature reminiscent of the Mediterranean, hang terracotta pots together on a sunny wall.*

ABOVE: *Terracotta is a traditional material used for garden pots and ornaments in formal settings. The texture and colour contrast well with the topiary, clipped hedging and gravel pathways, while the muted colours add to the restful atmosphere of this classical terrace.*

When fired, ceramic glazes undergo a metamorphosis, depending on the ingredients used, and gardeners can now select from a broad palette of shades and finishes to suit their taste. Some glaze colours are clear and vibrant, others subtle and earthy, and the character of the ornament is further influenced by the surface sheen – high gloss, or, with the addition of sand, almost matt with a rough texture.

Glazed pots have the advantage of being frost-proof, but always check for blistering before you buy. Unlike terracotta, they won't weather, so with the exception of the new bronze and pewter-look items, it may be harder to place them in a period setting. Jade green, dramatic black or lacquer red jars are often associated with Oriental style gardens. And vivid cobalt-blue containers are as popular in contemporary urban plots as they are in country or cottage idylls. Because of their reflective finish, large, glazed vessels, such as Chinese ginger jars, add a magical sparkle to shady corners, especially when associated with water. Resist the temptation to plant such containers every time; sometimes the uncluttered purity of line is the key to an objects decorative value.

Of course, your choice of glazed ceramic work isn't confined to pots and containers. There are ornamental objects such as spheres, smooth "floating" stones and oil lamps, as well

as animal figures. You may also come across Oriental-style stools or intricately designed mosaic table tops. Mosaics pre-date ancient Rome and are usually associated with floor and wall decoration, but with a few simple tools and the right kind of waterproof tile adhesive, you could create your own designs, either using manufactured tesserae or handmade shards snipped from frostproof tiles. As well as table tops, you could decorate terracotta pots and glassware, make ornamental hangings or even put your individual stamp on a lacklustre wall by designing a unique panel or plaque.

On a larger scale, use glazed, frostproof tiles to add colour and textural variation. A formal pool with a raised surround, finished with lustrous deep blue tiles, would be perfect for the centre of a Moorish-style courtyard garden, or black and white tiling could be arranged in a chequerboard motif.

Some tiles are so beautifully designed that you could use them individually as wall ornaments

metal

This extremely versatile group of materials has so many different forms and patinas – including stainless steel, wrought iron and verdigris – that the possibilities for garden decoration are almost limitless.

In the modern, minimalist or urban landscape, sculpture and furniture with a highly polished chrome or stainless steel finish is dramatic and eye-catching. Use it sparingly so as not to overwhelm the space, and keep the setting simple. The reflective surface will capture surrounding foliage and wall colours, adding to the ornamental effect, but mirror-effect sculpture can also look stunning set in a dark reflecting pool. In a shady spot, sheets of polished stainless steel may be attached to walls, helping to draw light into the space, or used freestanding, cut into curving abstract shapes. One of the easiest ways to give a futuristic feel to the garden is to set groups of tall, gleaming spiral plant supports into the border. You can also incorporate geometric topiary frames, painted in vivid shades, for their decorative outline.

For a softer look, suitable for more rural settings and cottage gardens, or to evoke a seaside feel with shingle and driftwood, restrict your colour scheme to the matt grey of containers made from galvanized steel, aluminium or zinc. Tall, traditional flower buckets are most effective when arranged in multiples, spaced equidistantly in a line. Their profile looks wonderful with the arching foliage of ornamental grasses or clipped box balls. Take care when planting up the buckets to ensure stability; alternatively, simply fill the buckets to the brim with pebbles.

Old watering cans, galvanized pails, tin baths and other household items can also assume a decorative role in the garden. For a contemporary look, plant them up with glossy green foliage, or for a seaside flavour use flowering plants and herbs in muted silvers and whites, greys and lavenders. Metal containers must be insulated on the inside before planting – they heat up rapidly in direct sun, cooking the root ball – and offer poor protection from extreme cold. Use layers of bubble plastic or polystyrene (Styrofoam) sheeting.

LEFT: *Plant support spirals may be used in a purely decorative way by setting one or more upright into a border. Amongst low planting, the effect can be like a series of water jets.*

RIGHT: *Modern galvanized containers are particularly effective when planted up with simple geometric topiary pieces. Don't forget to line the pot with insulating material first.*

BELOW: *Pieces of bronze sculpture with a weathered patina look very much at home in the garden but can be expensive. Look out for the cheaper bronze resin alternatives.*

Different kinds of metalwork are often associated with particular historic periods – for example, cast iron with the Victorian and Edwardian eras; lead with the 17th and 18th centuries, and gold leaf and copper verdigris with the Italian and French Renaissance. Some of the most romantic elements for the garden are made from wirework, which has strong associations with the Regency period. The fine filigree appearance of wirework plant pot stands, baskets and arbours is rivalled only by the scrolls and delicate floral and leaf motifs of top quality wrought iron. Original period pieces can be very expensive, but fortunately you can buy reproduction furniture, urns, vases and statuary, often made from cheaper, more lightweight materials such as fibreglass resin, cast aluminium, and even UV-resistant plastic.

The natural oxidation processes that occur on the surface of certain metals help to soften ornaments, making them appear more organic and in sympathy with the garden. Part of the charm of sculptural elements made from iron is that their appearance changes over time as the rust develops, revealing a surprising spectrum of colour. Large coppers salvaged from junk shops make excellent ornamental containers that weather to the characteristic greenish-blue of verdigris – lovely in a country or cottage setting.

The downside of wrought- and cast-iron, as well as non-galvanized wirework, is that it rusts if the paintwork is damaged, but don't let that put you off. Sometimes the charm of period pieces is the gentle decay that creates an air of faded elegance. If you would rather keep the rust at bay, you can periodically remove any loose flakes with a wire brush and re-coat the object with a proprietary metal paint that protects against oxidation.

Gold detailing, used sparingly, adds warmth and a feeling of opulence. Gold leaf is expensive but is more lustrous than gold paint or metallic powders. Unless you have had some practice in applying gold leaf, experiment first with the cheaper Dutch metal leaf. Apply directly to wooden finials, stone spheres or decorative metal work and protect with a clear sealant to prevent it from turning black. If the gold effect is too bright, antique with paints or partially rub off.

TOP: *Galvanized metal vessels have a relaxed utilitarian feel and they look just right planted up with simple cottage flowers.*

LEFT: *Given the right spot, a rusting cast-iron piece can add to the charm of a garden. If you prefer, coat the piece with anti-rust finish to protect against the elements.*

ABOVE: *This beautiful verdigris armillary sphere or celestial globe would make an eye-catching feature mounted on a stone pedestal at the centre of a formal herb or rose garden. Here, the interconnecting rings of the metal globe are strikingly offset by the long, spiky foliage of the phormiums and ornamental grasses.*

wood

Wood is a living, breathing material that is easily weathered and warm to the touch. Being a product of nature, it blends easily into the garden and is at home in both traditional and contemporary locations.

Wood is an extremely versatile material. It has an inherent beauty that is enhanced by the elements, and it need not be sawn, turned or smoothed by machine to be made ornamental. A piece of sinuous driftwood picked up from the seashore, bleached white by salt and worn smooth by wave action, can rival many abstract sculptures.

Tree stumps excavated from the ground, roots and all, can form the basis of a gothic grotto planted up with ferns and wild flowers, and log slices set at different heights, like organ pipes, make an impromptu sculpture, as well as casual seating for the wild garden. Some craftsmen work exclusively with trees that have been blown down in the wind or simply come to the end of their lives. The resultant sculptures and pieces of furniture are full of character because the natural shape of the wood and bark has been retained.

Substantial pieces of sawn timber can be difficult to obtain, but there are companies that deal with reclaimed wood, such as old house beams and railway sleepers. This has a suitably aged and weathered feel that is perfect for the garden. A simple bench seat made from a recycled beam mounted on stone blocks would harmonize beautifully with a Zen-style rock and gravel garden.

Outdoors, wood is often treated, but fresh paint can look too new for the surroundings, especially in country gardens. Paintwork can be made to look older by being distressed or sanded to reveal some of the grain or an underlying base coat. It also helps to use softer paint colours, such as a soft blue-grey. If wood is left untreated, it develops a gentle grey tone that is a million miles away from the harsh orange-brown of some preservatives. Different species have distinct bark and grain patterns, and depending on the density of the wood and presence of resins, some timbers, such as oak or Western red cedar, have an impressive natural durability.

LEFT: *Wooden furniture often has a sculptural quality. Here, this is emphasised further against a background of wooden decking.*

RIGHT: *These bench seats made from untreated wood match the relaxed mood of the area perfectly. For permanent outdoor use choose timber that has a natural resistance to rot, such as many of the hardwoods.*

BELOW: *A wooden birdhouse is a charming ornament, and it is essential if you want to attract birds to your garden. Providing food – such as nuts and seeds moulded into balls of lard – will ensure a good supply of feathered friends.*

Wood is less likely to be used in ultra-modern garden settings, where polished metal, coloured plastic and fabric furniture dominate, but simple designs in wood can help to create a softer, more relaxed feel. Treated softwoods are frequently used at the cheaper end of the market, but most are not as durable as hardwoods and need regular preservative treatment. There are some concerns about the use of tropical hardwood, most of which doesn't come from managed plantations, but species such as Iroko are considered acceptable. Temperate hardwoods, such as oak, elm and ash are also used, but these tend to be expensive. High quality marine plywood has helped to increase the decorative potential of wood. Sheets may be cut into intricate designs like spiders' webs or foliage for chair and bench backs. These cut-outs also make attractive panels for wall decoration. Trellis panels that create false perspective are a variation on the theme.

Wooden furniture has a reassuring solidity that helps it to look grounded and very much part of the landscape. Furniture styles vary, and some abstractly sculpted chairs and benches are nothing short of works of art: given the right setting, a well-designed bench or chair could easily take the place of an ornament or a piece of sculpture. We unconsciously relax when we see that there is somewhere to sit down, and so it

ABOVE LEFT: *Even though this furniture is made from raw wood, the simple curving lines add a contemporary note.*

ABOVE RIGHT: *This wooden console table was designed for conventional use indoors, but it has been weatherproofed and moved outside to the garden.*

LEFT: *In time, wood weathers to gentle grey and though this trellis obelisk is of a formal design, it looks mellow enough for a cottage garden.*

is a good idea to incorporate at least one piece of permanent seating into your garden design. Simple Shaker or Gothic-style furniture in untreated oak works well in country gardens, and while Lutyens-style benches are a trademark of formal Arts and Crafts gardens, their elegant, clean lines suit many periods. Greenwood and rustic furniture designs can be a little quirky, but their individualistic character suits cottage gardens. You will rarely find handcrafted pieces in your local garden centre, so if you are looking for something special, it is worth going to visit the studios and workshops of craftsmen and carpenters.

If you wanted to show some design flair, you could finish off garden structures such as pergolas and summer houses with carved wooden finials. Acorns work well in period settings, and for a touch of luxury, why not paint them gold.

Garden furniture made from raw, unpainted wood
blends easily with its organic surroundings

glass

The beauty of glass is its translucency. When light shines through an object made from this crystalline material it literally springs to life and, like metal, glass can be wrought into a myriad of shapes.

In the garden, glass glinting amongst the foliage adds a magical, otherworldly quality, and more and more contemporary designers are now using glass to create special effects. However, few off-the-peg garden ornaments are made from glass – it is usually considered too fragile, and in garden centres the nearest you are likely to find to glass is Perspex.

It is quite easy to make your own decorations by recycling attractive glass containers. Pale sea-green wine bottles or deep blue water bottles are particularly effective and may be set in niches, ranged on top of walls or turned upside down and part-buried to make an unusual border edging. For a more traditional feel seek out old carboys, demijohns and cloches from junk shops and antique emporiums. If you are looking for a seaside motif, why not go beachcombing and collect some wave-worn pieces of glass or acquire a clutch of coloured fishermen's floats. Chunky, recycled glass containers and glass bricks are inexpensive to experiment with and should survive the frosts if left outdoors for the winter.

Oversized blown-glass baubles have recently found favour with interior designers and are now available beyond the Christmas period. Hang them at different levels from a pergola or archway to catch the light at certain times of day. Mirrored gazing balls have a spellbinding quality, especially when positioned to reflect the surrounding garden. These are most effective raised off the ground on stone plinths or used as finials.

At night-time, glass lanterns are unquestionably romantic. You can give ordinary-looking jam jars a Moorish accent simply by painting them with gold and jewel-coloured stained glass paints available from craft shops. They make perfect holders for nightlights.

Whatever glass ornament you choose, remember to place it in such a way that it catches the light, and clean and polish it occasionally to maintain the lustrous sheen.

LEFT: *Glass chippings provide a glittering alternative to gravel and can be used to enhance the effectiveness of modern sculpture. It can be interesting to vary the texture of the chippings with glass beads or marbles*

RIGHT: *Abstract art like this would be relatively easy to position within the garden because the blue-green glass looks just like melting glacier ice. Keep it gleaming by rinsing off any debris with water.*

BELOW: *Stained glass hangings need to be positioned where you can see the light shining through them – from a pergola, perhaps, or an aperture in a wall or fence. Always site glass carefully to avoid accidental breakage.*

Modern landscape designers are always looking for novel materials and glass has proved particularly versatile. Recycled glass chippings make a refreshing alternative to gravel and stone aggregates, and as there are no sharp edges it is safe to walk on. It also works well as a lining for ornamental pools, with the pale blue-green version looking like crushed ice. Try mixing blue and green in abstract swirls or wave designs. An algal film will eventually dull the effect, but if the pool has a purely decorative function you can treat it with an algicide.

If you are feeling daring you could use bright cornflower blue chips as a base for plain terracotta pots or to mulch borders planted with bold architectural specimens, such as palms and phormiums: vivid shades are best used as occasional accents, so don't overdo it. Stick with evergreens to avoid the problem of leaf debris, and before you begin, peg down sheets of landscaping membrane to prevent contamination of the glass with soil. If you need large quantities, buying direct from the recycling factories will be more economical.

Use coloured chippings to mulch pots, containers, and narrow borders at the base of walls and raised beds. Hollow or solid "pebbles" made from glass or acrylic can be used outdoors as textural contrast, highlighting ornamental features or adding ribbons of colour within shingle and gravel surfaces.

ABOVE FROM LEFT: *Blown glass bubbles mix with shells, pebbles and driftwood to conjure a seaside feel. Recycled glass chippings for landscaping come in several shades, but blue-green has a naturalistic appeal. Being so robust, glass brick may be used as paving with a contemporary accent.*

LEFT: *Glass bricks let chinks of light into the garden without affecting privacy. Here they are used to enhance a fountain-like mosaic.*

It is not unusual to see stained glass panels in the doors and windows of a house but it is unusual in a garden setting, and so all the more intriguing when used effectively. You don't have to be artistically gifted. Simply fix two or three coloured glass panels into a heavy-duty trellis screen and let the light do the rest – instant abstract art! Strong primary colours work well, though opalescent sheets are lovely as a contrast to soft pastel plantings. You can also suspend small stained-glass hangings from tree branches with wire, but space them far enough apart to make sure they are not able to collide on a windy day.

To fill larger apertures, it is safer and easier to use coloured acrylic or Plexi-glass sheeting, available from specialist suppliers. One of the most effective shades for use overhead, for instance for roof panels in a pergola, is deep rich blue. Everything is bathed in coloured light and the effect is very calming.

As far back as medieval times, man has been experimenting with light shining though coloured glass

stone

Amidst the ever-changing backdrop of the garden, the apparent strength and solidity of stonework engenders an air of calmness, and natural weathering can make stone appear much older than it is.

Garden stonework ranges from urns, sundials and decorative wall friezes to troughs, containers and pots. The styles are equally diverse, from classically inspired statuary for the formal garden to a rough-hewn object for a rural vegetable plot. If you had a garden inspired by the medieval period, you could even add Gothic gargoyles for a touch of theatre. However, it pays to be selective as the subject and quality of stone can leave much to be desired. It is far more preferable from a visual standpoint to invest in one large quality item than to scatter several lesser ornaments around.

You can buy original period pieces from antiques dealers and auction houses, but in architectural salvage yards you will find cheaper pieces of stone masonry, such as pillars and archways and even old fireplaces, that can make unusual and effective garden ornaments. These elements need not be perfect; in fact, pieces of a broken pillar could form part of a folly and help to create a feeling of mystery.

Reconstituted stone, concrete and stone resin elements make acceptable substitutes for the real thing; they weather easily and are usually cheaper and more widely available. New stone looks harsh but it can be aged with chemicals available from the stone manufacturers. Acrylic paints may also be used to define relief patterns more clearly, darkening the crevices and stippling the raised parts to create the effect of weathering. Concoctions of manure or natural yogurt also help to speed up colonization by algae, mosses and lichens.

Contemporary stone and concrete sculpture is much harder to come by than classically inspired elements, but this is gradually changing, especially with regard to fountain design. Seal concrete pools and water sculptures with a proprietary agent to prevent lime leaching into the water, as this could affect the health of any fish or pondlife.

ABOVE: *Stone wall plaques bearing symbols and sayings add a timeless quality and work particularly well when surrounded by a covering of ivy.*

RIGHT: *This contemporary sculpture, with its simple lines, has been placed in a minimalist setting so that the viewer can contemplate it without distraction. A stone sphere would also work well here.*

LEFT: *Classically inspired stone statuary needs careful siting to avoid the results appearing ostentatious or overly sentimental. This cherubic figure, half hidden amongst plants, illustrates the value of proper framing. A subtle approach like this is far more in keeping with an average informal garden.*

The stylized Zen rock and gravel gardens, or *karesansui*, show how natural stone pieces can be just as significant in the landscape as shrubs and trees. The groupings of stones, which are positioned with great care and artistry, are broadly triangular in outline, a shape that is both stable and dynamic, and can represent islands in a sea or lake, mountain peaks emerging from the cloud layer or more surreal concepts. Even if this minimalist style doesn't appeal, the decorative value of natural stone shouldn't be overlooked. It works beautifully in a relaxed, somewhat naturalistic setting, especially in association with water, and individual pieces can have the effect of anchoring the surrounding planting or emphasizing features of the ground plan. For example, you could use an arrangement of large stones at the mouth of a garden path. Single standing stones also have tremendous dramatic potential and act like abstract art, provided the surrounding space is kept simple and uncluttered.

Like wood, different types of stone have a unique signature. Limestone and sandstone are porous, weather easily and soon become colonized by mosses and lichens. At the other end of the scale is granite, which is noted for being impervious to the elements. A carved granite water bowl is a traditional element in the Japanese tea garden, but you could use stone bowls in a far more contemporary setting because their simple shapes have a timeless quality. Bowls made from reconstituted stone are somewhat less expensive but can look just as authentic. Slate is another useful form of stone and, unlike granite, it splits readily into smooth, thin sheets. The darkness of slate is emphasized by rain or when it is splashed by a fountain, leaving pieces gleaming like polished leather.

Stone cairns make a strong visual statement and these may be a more practical proposition if it is difficult or impossible to manoeuvre very large pieces within the confines of your outdoor room. Like standing stones, cairns add an air of ancient mysticism to gardens. They can be built quite easily using flat rocks, such as pieces of slate or limestone. On a smaller scale, smooth rounded cobbles can also be piled on top of one another to form cone-shaped sculptures.

ABOVE: *This simple cairn is reminiscent of a snail shell. Try grouping cairns of different sizes to create abstract sculpture.*

LEFT: *Standing stones or monoliths made from rough-hewn slate and other rock types make striking natural sculptures and work well in country or urban settings.*

TOP: *In the Japanese tea garden water and stone form a natural partnership. Although granite is traditionally used for items such as lanterns and water basins, porous stone is readily colonized by algae and mosses that help make the garden feel more established.*

water

When sculpture is combined with moving water, the results can be breathtaking, the sparkling droplets often seeming to animate the figure. The tranquil serenity of still water can be equally atmospheric.

Water is deeply fascinating and it always adds something unique to a garden setting. Whether it is the contemplative calm of still water or the invigorating, purifying quality of rushing, bubbling streams and fountains, we seem instinctively to derive comfort from being near water, and this makes it a virtually endless source of inspiration for beautiful and satisfying ornamental garden features.

Wall fountains with underground reservoirs or raised pools can be a space-saving option for town gardens and terraces. A spouting lion's head or a mask from classical mythology would suit a courtyard garden, but a stepped cascade might have more impact in a contemporary setting.

Whether it be a simple stone basin or a naturalistic pond filled with fish, there are numerous ways to contain water. In a limited space, self-contained water features are ideal. These consist of a reservoir from which the water is recirculated via an electric pump, usually topped by some kind of ornamental structure. All the elements for do-it-yourself construction will be available at garden centres and aquatic stores, but if you are in doubt about connecting the electric pump, you should contact a professional electrician.

If you want to incorporate water as a focus for the garden but are looking for a more contemporary feel, the answer is to go for a pool with a simple outline, perhaps an ellipse or plain rectangle. The pool need not be large to achieve the effect. If possible, site it out in the open so that the water surface reflects the sky and cloudscape. The eye is immediately drawn by glinting water, and it can be a mistake to try to overdo ornamental detail: let the pool speak for itself and exercise a little restraint. For an Oriental theme, you might place a stone lantern or a sculpture of a sacred crane at the water's edge. Within a geometrically shaped pool in a modern garden, an abstract piece made from mirrored metal could be perfect.

LEFT: *Reproducing a naturalistic waterfall or cascade using rocks and pebbles can be difficult. Play around with the elements until the water falls as you would like it to.*

ABOVE: *A formal geometric pond with Oriental overtones makes a stunning focal point in any garden setting, but it will have particular impact in smaller spaces.*

If the sight and sound of moving water is important to you, then a fountain is the ideal choice. Some fountains are decorated with sculpture, while for others it is the movement and play of the water itself that is the main attraction. Both types of fountain are possible, even if space is limited and you only have room for a small container.

Abstract metal, ceramic or glass water sculptures work well in contemporary urban plots, where the layout is minimalist and architectural. In period settings, while you could use statues inspired by myth and legend, non-figurative pieces or simple water jets are often easier to accommodate. Rustic, workaday features are ideally suited to cottage garden settings. You could use a large millstone as a sculptural element, or an old ceramic sink filled with cobbles could be pressed into service as the reservoir for a wall fountain.

Rock and water form an easy partnership and in a relaxed plot, away from the formality of the house, rocky cascades, pebble streams and natural springs make serene points of focus and contemplation. Sandstone, limestone, granite and slate are all popular types of rock to use in water gardens.

Japan provides much of the inspiration for naturalistic rock and water landscapes. In particular, there are the gardens that surround the tea houses, which are known as the dewy path or *roji*, as well as stroll gardens. Both kinds are characterized by narrow winding paths reminiscent of mountain trails; moss-covered rocks set amongst the plantings; still reflecting pools – the margins softened with ornamental sedges and water irises – and narrow streams crossed by stepping-stones or rustic timber bridges. Of course, landscapes such as these are much easier to bring to effect when there is an existing watercourse, but following the Japanese example, you could create the impression of a stream or cascade simply by laying down a ribbon of cobbles, pebbles or slate shards, punctuated by larger pieces of rough-hewn rock. More ambitious water projects must be thought through carefully, perhaps with professional advice, to avoid problems in construction and aftercare. It is worth remembering that even modest pools can generate huge amounts of spoil, and this has to be disposed of or somehow worked into the design plan.

TOP: *Fantasy themes seem to work particularly well with water, and this sculpture of enchanted fish would suit many different locations.*

RIGHT: *The dominant placing and use of walling stones has created an individual water feature, which makes a powerful statement in what is otherwise an informal garden.*

ABOVE: *Water is pumped through the centre of this millstone, falling over the sides to the reservoir below.*

foliage

Plants act like living sculptures and their architectural outline can be just as dramatic as man-made art. With a little judicious pruning, a pleasing shape can be coaxed out of quite ordinary garden specimens.

Using sculptural plants successfully is about scale and textural contrast. When the majority of plants are fine-textured and low-growing, an architectural specimen doesn't have to be enormous to stand out. On the other hand, if your garden is crowded, a plant would need a very strong profile and a suitable backdrop to act as a focal point.

Think of the scene your chosen plant brings to mind and add to the effect with appropriate propping. Specimens with bold sword-shaped leaves radiating out like a fountain spray are theatrical and bring to mind hot, dry landscapes. For a Riviera touch, plant them in large terracotta pots and set against a white-washed backdrop. For a Mexican or Moorish courtyard, paint the backdrop with yellow ochre or cobalt blue.

The sort of plants that make good sculpture tend to originate from warmer climes and may need overwintering in frost-free conditions before moving pots onto the terrace or bedding specimens out in the borders for the summer. Typical examples include exotic ginger lilies (*Hedychium*), angel's trumpets (*Brugmansia*) and Indian shot (*Canna*). There are spectacular varieties, such as phormiums, yuccas, bamboos and Pampas grass, that will grow outdoors all year round in cool temperate zones, as well as borderline hardy types, including cordylines, tree ferns, the Chusan fan palm (*Trachycarpus fortunei*) and Japanese banana (*Musa basjoo*) that can be nurtured in the warmth of city gardens or against sunny, sheltered walls.

TOP LEFT: *This potted cordyline makes an eye-catching focal point.*

LEFT: *These stately, white flowered tobacco plants (*Nicotiana sylvestris) *can grow up to 1.5m (5ft) tall and have impressive paddle-shaped leaves.*

RIGHT: *Plants like this* Agave americana *add a touch of exotica to the summer garden. Overwinter tender specimens in pots in a frost-free greenhouse or conservatory, and water succulents and other drought-tolerant plants sparingly.*

topiary

Close-clipped geometric topiary shapes act almost like carved stonework and masonry. They stand out strongly when set amongst diaphanous flowers and foliage, and really hold their own close to buildings.

The ancient art of topiary is a form of sculpture in which the medium is living plants. There are several different forms and traditions, from the so-called cloud pruning of the East to the formal geometric shapes that were popular during the Italian and French Renaissance periods. Topiary can involve whole hedges or individual trees and shrubs, and the style of sculpting can be anything from abstract and free form to rigidly geometric or figurative. Topiary frames allow complex shapes to be created rapidly, using quick-growing species and evergreen climbers like ivy.

Simple shapes fit into gardens of any historical period and, given the right setting or style of container, they are perfectly at home in contemporary landscapes. Animal figures and quirky asymmetric forms work well in relaxed country or cottage-style gardens. One of the wonderful aspects of creating topiary is that you have the opportunity to experiment with sculpture – any mistakes will soon grow back.

ABOVE: *A sphere is one of the easiest shapes to create. Stand above the piece and flip your shears over so that the blades follow the curve.*

TOP RIGHT: *With features such as a traditional herb garden or herbaceous border, topiary can be used to establish a period feel and may be shaped into walls, buttresses and finials. Here solid obelisks make an excellent contrast with frothy flowers.*

RIGHT: *Classic shapes, such as mop-headed standards, globes and spirals, are often used in pairs to add weight and importance to doors and entrance ways in the garden. Box topiary prefers a sheltered, semi-shaded position and even watering to keep the roots cool and moist. Though terracotta looks more traditional, the plants will do better in glazed ceramic containers.*

organics

Objects gathered from the natural world have a sculptural form that is subtly ornamental. Seashells
are a classic example, but dried seed pods, fir cones and fruits can also be collected for decoration.

Natural treasures such as stones, cones, driftwood, acorns and seashells can all be bought in the shops, but this is somehow missing the point. Instead, make the most of objects collected as souvenirs from trips to the coast or walks in the country, and use them as simple ornaments to add a personal note to your garden.

Exquisitely formed seashells can be embedded into the ground to make a decorative edging for a border or pathway, or you could set them out in rows on a ledge to be viewed in isolation. Smaller shells, such as slate-blue mussels, can be used as an attractive pot mulch, or threaded on to twine to make mobiles and garlands. Large fir cones may be piled high in baskets or wired together to make wall hangings, and door wreaths can be woven from any number of natural materials, including dried flower heads, leaves, berries and feathers.

Some materials can be wired or glued together and stapled on to gateposts, pergola pillars or fencing, or even used to create a rustic façade for an outdoor building such as a garden shed; for larger areas, try attaching pieces of cork bark.

ABOVE: *Large scallop shells make*
a pretty edging for a flower border.
They could also be arranged in a
pattern and set into mortar to make
a wall decoration.

TOP RIGHT: *Beachcombing*
can uncover some wonderful items –
feathers, driftwood, shells and even
fossils. Group them to add a
seaside flavour to the garden.

RIGHT: *Wreaths and garlands*
don't have to be complex.
You could simply twist together
the flexible coloured stems of
dogwood. If you use a metal frame,
wire on evergreen foliage or dried
materials as a background for key
elements, such as long-lasting fruits,
berries and seed heads.

wicker

Willow and other pliable stems have been woven for thousands of years as household objects, but more recently, willow sculpture and other woven structures have come into their own as inspired garden art.

Willow weavings can be made to fit any particular style or area. There is no limit on size and shape, and even a gap in a hedge or fence could be filled with a woven willow screen that has been made to measure. Woven animal figures look stylized and original, and, being organic and full of imperfections, they are appropriate in rustic or rural plots.

There is no reason why you couldn't weave your own sculptural elements. Use either willow obtained in bundles from craft centres and soaked beforehand, or fresh willow stems and other flexible prunings, such as dogwood. Start with simple decorative screens, plant support frames and obelisks and progress gradually to other, more complex shapes.

Wicker structures don't last long – up to eight years at best – but their ephemeral and constantly changing character is part of their appeal. However, live willow will often strike and structures may suddenly spring into growth. This can be an advantage if you want the structures to blend in with the garden, for example, to shape a tunnel for children to play in.

TOP LEFT: *This elegant plant support mirrors the design of a metal obelisk. Simple wigwams bound with bands of wicker are much easier to construct.*

LEFT: *Abstract willow weavings can be used to make decorative screens and gap fillers, blending readily with surrounding vegetation.*

ABOVE: *It takes practice and a considerable amount of skill to weave a convincing animal shape such as this pig. For most people, objects such as this will have to be bought from a specialist craftsman.*

pigment

Applying a colour or pigment to an object or a piece of furniture can transform it into a decorative element, and this is an inexpensive but satisfying way to be creative, even on a tight budget.

Although it is not a material in the true sense of the word, a pigment can be considered as such because of its ability to transform ordinary objects into novel garden features.

Sometimes all that is needed to make an ornament more eye-catching is to contrast it with its surroundings – a blue painted bench in the middle of a yellow border, for example. The application of a couple of coats of paint can also make an everyday item appear less utilitarian. An ordinary metal bucket or watering-can could be given a fresh look with a coat of forget-me-not blue or sunflower yellow, and it immediately becomes a feature in a modern potager or cottage garden. Another example of this trick is the olive oil can that is transformed into an attractive plant pot.

You can be subtle or outrageous with the shades you select. It's a matter of taste, but don't shy away from making your own modern art or putting a fresh slant on a classic garden feature, such as an obelisk, gateway or fence.

ABOVE: *Sometimes the simplest ideas work best. These cans were painted blue to tie in with the setting, and planted with marigolds to make a stunning display.*

RIGHT: *Painting an old gardening trug with woodstain will provide a splash of colour in the garden.*

TOP RIGHT: *Bright colours can be an excellent way of enlivening a dull area, especially in places where planting is difficult, such as a paved backyard that doesn't get much natural sunlight.*

fabrics & textiles

Bringing fabrics into the garden is a way of linking indoor and outdoor rooms and creating a feeling of luxury and opulence. You needn't spend a fortune as remnants and off-cuts can often be bought very cheaply.

Fabric throws, hangings and cushions may be used to inject colour and texture into a relatively plain, simple space such as an evergreen garden, paved courtyard or pool area, taking the place of seasonal flowers. Make impromptu seating with cushions set along a retaining wall, or cast a bright cloth over an outdoor trestle table to lift a dining area ready for entertaining. If possible, house garden textiles in a convenient weatherproof cupboard for easy access.

Fabrics and textiles are also a very effective way of adding theatre-like drama and fantasy to a garden area. Temporary tent-like structures or draped canopies of luxurious fabrics may be used to conjure up an Arabian Nights theme for an outdoor party. For an atmosphere of romance, hang sheer fabrics, such as muslin or voile, over a simple metal-frame. At night, decorate the frame with tiny white fairy lights.

The enormous variety of fabrics available means that they can be used to create any number of subtler themes. For a maritime flavour, suspend robust canvas fabric on wire hawsers to make screens and windbreaks. Canvas may also be sculpted into surreal, sail-like awnings that function practically but also perform as pieces of outdoor art. One-off structures like these must be commissioned directly from sail manufacturers or ship's chandlers. Off-the-peg parasols can also make stylish focal points for the terrace. Large wooden-framed parasols clothed in cream canvas have an elegant colonial feel, while deep blue or green fabric shades suit modern locations. If you have a pergola, you could loop translucent fabrics below the crossbars to cut out the sun's glare and create pools of coloured light.

For a taste of the East or to decorate a space dedicated to mind, body and spirit, you might use pennants or prayer flags or make vibrant Thai-style banners of fabric and bamboo canes to flutter in the breeze.

ABOVE: *Floor cushions create an atmosphere conducive to lounging and relaxation. As shown in this shady retreat, they can give an Eastern feel to a garden, and are perfect for dressing a sunny deck.*

RIGHT: *Hammocks are the ultimate in chill-out furniture for those lazy summer days. If you don't have a conveniently spaced tree, try stringing up a hammock between a wall and a pergola post using securely fixed hooks.*

LEFT: *Fluttering pennants and flags are an imaginative way to add a splash of colour and can be made cheaply and easily with material scraps and long, flexible bamboo canes. Use fabric paints to add your own motifs.*

index

PICTURE CREDITS
The publishers would like
to thank the following
photographers for their
contributions to this book:
Peter Anderson p54b, 55;
Jonathan Buckley p50 RHS
Chelsea Flower Show (1999);
Michelle Garrett p29t, 39t,
41l, 59br, 61br; © **Jenny
Hendy** p44, 47l Catherina
Rhodes (owner), 47r; **Simon
McBride** p19tl, 19tr, 21, 33b;
35r; **Peter McHoy** p58br;
James Mitchell p4–5, 16t,
16b; **Debbie Patterson** p7b,
13l, 14t, 14b, 15, 18tl, 19br,
20t, 20b, 22, 23, 25, 26t, 26b,
28, 29b, 30–31, 38, 42, 43r, 48,
53, 59l, 61tr, 63r; **Spike Powell**
p59tr, 61tl, 62; © **Juliette Wade**
p2; **Jo Whitworth** p1 Heale
House, 3 RHS Tatton Park
(1999), Alan Gardner (designer),
6 Julia van den Bosch
(owner), 7t Christina Oates
(designer), 8 Le Manoir aux
Quart' Saisons, 10, 11 RHS
Chelsea Flower Show (1999),
George Carter (designer),
12 Forge Cottage, 13r East
Ruston Old Vicarage, 17
Joan Spirals (designer), 18bl,
18r West Green House, 24
RHS Hampton Court,
D. Fairweather (designer), 27,
32, 33t Ilford Manor, 34, 35l

Heale House, 35c, 36, 37l, 37r
Diana Yakely (designer), 39b
RHS Tatton Park (1999),
40 The Hannah Peschar
Sculpture Garden/Anthony
Paul (designer), 41r, 43
RHS Chelsea Flower Show
(1999), 45l Julia van den
Bosch (owner), 45r The
Hannah Peschar Sculpture
Garden/Anthony Paul
(designer), 46, 47c, 49l New
Art Centre Sculpture Park
and Gallery/Meichel Watts
(designer), 49r Brook Hall,
Essex, 51t Ilford Manor,
51b, 52, 54t RHS Hampton
Court (1999), 56t Ilford
Manor, 56b Judy Wiseman,
57 RHS Chelsea Flower
Show, 58l College Cross,
Islington, London, 58tr
Old Vicarage, 60tl, 60bl
The Hannah Peschar
Sculpture Garden/Anthony
Paul (designer), 63t, 64b
Gay Wilson (designer).